CONTENTS

Dedication

To my beloved parents Harvey and Lucille, who were and are to this day, the most supportive parents anyone could ask for, thank you for instilling in me the knowledge and awareness of money management and the concepts of saving. To my dad, for inspiring me while growing up by sitting at the kitchen table night after night writing out our household budget on that yellow lined paper. To my mom, for being a constant quiet support system whenever anything in my life was going wrong.

To my son, Cory, for being the inspiration behind creating this book. I wanted a way to explain all of these concepts and strategies for you to use throughout your lifetime.

To my fiancé, Brian, who came along and became my biggest fan supporting me in every endeavor that I pursue and making me feel consistently loved.

Introduction

Money – We all need it to live. How you manage, spend and invest it can make a huge impact on your life but very few schools teach money management adequately or at all. Unfortunately, the Pythagorean Theorem and how to diagram sentences will not help you as you enter adulthood and all of the money responsibilities that go along with that. Just because you succeeded in high school or college does not mean you will succeed in life. Young adults are taught many things in school, but simple home economic concepts like creating and maintaining a budget are often overlooked. Without a plan, it's nearly impossible to meet the savings goals individuals and families need to reach their financial freedom.

But where do I start, you may ask? How do I create a simple household spending plan? How do I use credit responsibly? What does it even mean to invest? I am going to take the opportunity to answer those questions and a few more. The goal of this book is to explain the basics of household budgeting. This includes showing you why savings are important and how and why you should monitor your credit and credit score. Whether you are 15 or 50, this book will get you started into personal money management and help clarify the sometimes confusing financial jargon that you may encounter.

Okay . . . Let's go!

Chapter 1 -- Spend Less Than You Have – It Doesn't Have to be Complicated

It's kind of like the basics of dieting. In order to lose weight, you have to burn more calories than you consume. Well, in this case, you have to spend less money than you earn in order to have money left to save, invest or do other activities you enjoy. You know these things instinctively but you have to get to the point where you not only know them, but do them. So, how do you get to that point? You manage your finances with a Budget.

What is a Budget?

Uh-Oh, the dreaded 'B' word. Does the thought of a budget send you running for the hills assuming that it will be really hard, it's too much to do or you will have to give up everything you love to do? Nothing could be further from the truth. To make this a little easier to digest, let's call it a spend plan. That way you don't have to think of it as a punishment. A **spend plan** is simply a way to make the most out of your money and reach your financial goals. Much better right?

You can start off with some really simple principles to get your spend plan going and get a simple savings plan underway. There are various kinds of spend plans, but for the purposes of this book we are explaining *household spend plans*.

A household spend plan shows you where you are and how to get where you want to be. It generally consists of:

Income- What you have coming in and the source (i.e., job, gifts, investments, etc.)

Expenses- How much money you spend and where it goes (i.e., Rent, Food, etc.)

It's a helpful tool to help you prioritize your spending and manage your money—no matter how much or how little you have. It is also the key to financial freedom and stress free living, but more on that later.

Work on a Plan; Know Your 'Why'

This doesn't have to be some deep soul searching activity. You know your why all the time without even realizing it. When you plan your wardrobe for the next day you know your why (your end goal is going to work or school). You don't plan to get dressed and just stand around in your house staring at the ceiling. It's done with your why in mind. That's all I'm asking you to do. When you begin writing (or typing) your spend plan, pick a goal or two that you're trying to achieve. It may be you are tired of having more month than money or you may be interested in saving to purchase anything from a cell phone to a home of your own. It's ok if you discover that you have more month than money. That's just a flag to let you know you need to make some changes in how you are spending your money. Whatever your individual case may be, begin your plan with your 'why' in mind.

Mandatory and Discretionary Expenses

This is just a very formal label for very normal things. The difference between mandatory and discretionary expenses become important when creating your spend plan. *Mandatory Expenses* are bills that have to be paid on a regular basis like rent, mortgage payment, property taxes, commuting expenses, groceries and utilities. Insurance premiums, childcare costs and other costs that help individuals maintain health and earn income are considered mandatory. Saving money for the future should be considered critical and listed under mandatory as well. *Discretionary Expenses* are optional bills such as premium cable, jewelry, eating out at restaurants, and expensive clothing. Vacations, clubs and movies are also considered discretionary spending. If you're looking to understand your spending patterns or tone down your spending, look at your bank statements or credit card statements to find these non-essential discretionary spending items. You will probably be surprised at how much you spend on discretionary non-essential items. I'm not by any means suggesting that you have absolutely no fun. Oh, the horror! We all need fun in our lives but you have to go back and check your 'why' (what are your goals?) to know if you're on track with how much you're spending and how much you have left on a monthly basis.

Track Spending

Now you can start to put what you've learned so far on paper. Track your income and expenses in a spending plan. Pen and paper are still very accurate; jot it down on a piece of paper that you can keep with you. Electronic budgeting can make your job a bit easier by keeping running totals and doing the math for you. I tend to use the pen and paper method. So, let's get started. . **Step 1 - *Gather all of your documents*** – Just to name a few below:

- o Income
  - Paycheck
  - Gifts received
  - Interest earned bank statements
  - Side work

- Dividends (if you don't know dividends, don't worry -we'll cover that later)
    - Expenses
        - All bills
        - Groceries
        - Medical copays and medication
        - Work expenses (transportation, parking, gas)
        - Clothing and accessories
        - Gifts and Holidays
        - Spending money

You will want to further break this down into planned vs. actual amounts. What you expect vs. what the income and expenses actually were. Sometimes we spend more or less than we think we will. (See sample budget below)

Step 2 - *Categorize*

This is just finding out exactly where your money is going and if any adjustments are necessary. You can create categories similar to the ones below:

- Home
    - Rent or Mortgage
    - Property Taxes
    - Home Owners Association
- Utilities
    - Electricity
    - Gas

- - Phone
  - Cable
  - Family
    - Day Care
    - School Lunch
    - Extracurricular Activities
  - Auto
    - Car Payment
    - Gas
    - Insurance
    - Repairs
  - Debt Payments
    - Credit cards
    - Student Loans
    - Subscriptions
  - Health
    - Doctor visits
    - Prescription medication
  - Food
    - Groceries
    - Dining out
  - Personal
    - Entertainment
    - Clothing
    - Hair cuts
    - Spending money
    - Giving/donations
  - Savings
    - Emergency Fund
    - Big Ticket Items
    - Investments

The categories above can be further broken down into mandatory vs. discretionary expenses.

Step 3 - *Set up your spreadsheet and enter the amounts*:

For the pay period covering September 15 – September 30

Description	Mandatory/ Discretionary	Due Date	Planned Amount	Actual Amount	Paid
Annual Income			75,000		
Bi-Weekly Income			3,125		
401(k)	M		125		
Taxes	M	1/1/2016	900		
Health Insurance	M		75		
Automatic Ha Ha Savings Acct.	D		100		
Bi-weekly Net Income			1925		
Rent/ Mortgage	M	10/1-10/5/15	500		X
Property Taxes	M	1/1/2016	75		
Home Insurance	M	1/1/2016	40		X
Electric	M	10/13/2015	80		X
Water	M	11/30/2015	30		
Car Maintenance	M	10/5/2015	75		X
Phone	M	10/2/2015	30		
Car	M	10/30/2015	150		
Gas	M		60		X
Car Insurance	M	10/20/2015	60		
Groceries	M		70		X
Student Loan	M	10/9/2015	125		X
Big Ticket Item (Big Screen TV)	D		100 (*you will have saved $1,200 in one year to pay for the TV in cash*)		
Spending Money	D		80		
Church Giving			30		
Dining Out/Movies	D		100		
Christmas Fund	D		25 (*equates to $600 per year*)		
Investment Fund	D		100		
Total Expenses			1730		
Remaining			*195*		

For the pay period covering October 1 – October 15

*all amounts and dates are made up

Description	Mandatory/ Discretionary	Due Date	Planned Amount	Actual Amount	Paid
Annual Income			75,000		
Bi-Weekly Income			3,125		
401(k)	M		125		
Taxes	M	1/1/2016	900		
Health Insurance	M		75		
Automatic Savings Acct.	D		100		
Bi-weekly Net Income			1925		
Rent/ Mortgage	M	11/1-11/5/15	500		X
Property Taxes	M	1/1/2016	38		
Home Insurance	M	1/1/2016	40		X
Cable	D	10/24/2015	80		X
Internet	M	10/24/2015	30		X
Clothing	D		75		
Haircuts	D		30		
Car	M	10/30/2015	150		X
Gas	M		60		X
Insurance	M	10/20/2015	60		
Groceries	M		70		X
Prescriptions	M		25		
Credit Card	M	10/28/2015	150 (minimum payment is $60)		
Christmas Fund	D		25 (equates to $600 per year)		
Spending Money	D		80		
Summer Vacation	D		90 (if you save this amount per month, you will have saved $1,080 over a 12-month period)		
Investment Fund	D		100		
Misc. Splurge money	D		100		
Total Expenses			1703		
Remaining			222		

The light blue shaded areas represent amounts that usually remain the same if you have steady employment. The pink shaded areas represent amounts that are split in half since we are demonstrating a two week or bi-weekly pay period (i.e., mortgage is $1,000 monthly but we deduct $500 out of a two pay period month). The green shaded areas represent amounts that are only due one or two times per year so those costs are divided by either 12 months or 6 months. (i.e., Property tax is $900 for the year, it equates to $75 per month or approximately $38 per pay period). You still have to take $75 out of each pay period to ensure you have the money when it is due. The remaining expenses are placed onto one pay period or another based on what date they are due. Again, the goal is to spend less than your income so you will have money left over to save and invest.

You can make a spreadsheet similar to this for every pay period and update the amounts as necessary (if you are proficient in Microsoft Excel, you can set it up to complete the calculations for you). That way you can take a look back and see where your money went for the pay period/month/year and you can make any changes, especially if you have more month than money, to ensure you are working toward your savings, debt repayment and purchasing goals.

Step 4 – *Trim Discretionary Spending*

You can now see where your money is going and you may have discovered that you are spending entirely too much on dining out, clothing, or entertainment. You can begin to control your spending habits in these areas and move money ordinarily for those things into paying off credit card debt, saving for big ticket items you want, saving for emergencies or saving for investment purposes. Additionally, if you find you have a little extra leftover, you can set up a *direct deposit* from your paycheck to an additional **savings account** or investment account.

Types of Accounts

As you begin to get your finances in order, consider various accounts in which to hold your money. There are many types of accounts and features to choose from.

Checking Account – this is the most commonly used bank account because it offers easy access to your money. You can either write a check to transfer money from your account or use a debit or ATM card to withdraw or transfer funds. There are many options to consider when choosing a checking account, such as basic checking, student checking or interest-bearing checking. The best accounts are free. While they may not offer interest on your money, they also do not have monthly fees or balance requirements. They may, however, require you to have *direct deposit* set up from your job. **_Direct deposit_** is the electronic transfer of a payment directly from the account of the payer (your job) to your bank account. Most employers offer, and some employers require employees to get direct deposit.

Savings Account – this is a low to no risk account that allows you to collect interest, at a rate determined by your bank or credit union, on funds you're saving for the future. Interest rates can be compounded on a daily, weekly, monthly or annual basis. Interest on savings accounts is usually compounded daily and paid monthly. _Compounded interest_ is when the bank pays you interest on the money they've paid you in interest! That means that if your account earns one percent interest, then each day 1/365th of that one percent of the amount of money you have in your savings account is then added to your total. Below is the calculation:

Daily compounding = Principal (1 + interest rate/365)365 = (daily compounded amount)

Savings accounts are designed to provide users with an easy way to access funds but also come with a variety of terms and benefits. Some require monthly service fees, minimum opening deposits and varied rates of interest. Please do a comparison of types of accounts as well as different institutions such as banks vs. credit unions to realize the best choice for you. You can do this comparison by viewing the websites of most banks and credit unions.

Money Market Account – this is an account similar to a savings account but with it comes a requirement to maintain a higher balance to avoid a monthly fee. Instead of having fixed interest rates, these accounts have interest rates that vary (adjust) with the money markets. The rates are usually better with higher balances.

Individual Retirement Account (IRA) – this is a type of savings account that is designed to help you save for retirement and offers many tax advantages. *Yes You! Even if you are 18 with your first job, you want a retirement account. You will be glad when you reach an age you can't even imagine right now!* These accounts are especially useful if your employer does not offer retirement benefits or 401(k)s. There are two types of IRAs: *Traditional IRA* is where you pay the taxes on the back end (when you withdraw the money in retirement). *Roth IRA* is where you pay the taxes on the front end but there are no taxes on the back end, when you withdraw.

Certificate of Deposit (CD) – this is a type of savings account that allows you to invest your money at a set interest rate for a pre-set period of time. They are different from regular savings accounts in that the CD has a specific, fixed term (often monthly, three months, six months, or one to five years) and, usually, a fixed interest rate. It is intended that the CD be held until maturity, at which time the money may be withdrawn together with the accrued interest. The interest rates are normally higher than regular savings accounts because you are essentially restricting your own access to your money for the length specified by the CD. If you withdraw money from the CD before the term is over, you will incur a penalty (charge).

If You Still Live at Home

Don't panic. I know all of this might sound like a lot to understand. It really isn't. It's really this simple:

A budget, or spending plan, will help you cover all your needs, wants, expenses, and savings goals. It requires three things:

- Knowing how much money you spend
- Knowing your savings goals
- Managing your money

Let's look at a sample budget on a smaller scale:

Weekly Spend Plan

Money	How Much Do I Have?	Where did it come from?
Paycheck	$195	Working at the mall
Birthday Money	$100	Grandparents
Total Money	$295	All money added up

Stuff I Want to Buy	How Much Does it Cost?	Why I need it?
New Cell Phone	$200	Don't need it. Want it.
Transportation to Work	$50	Get to work to make more money.
What all of it Costs	$250	Everything I want to buy added up
Do I Have Enough? (Money – Cost)	$295-$250 = $45	Yes, I have enough and I have $45 left over to save in a bank account.

In this example, you do have enough money to get what you want **BUT** you have to decide whether the cell phone is that important to you to spend mostly all of the money you have on it or would you like to wait and save money from the next two or three paychecks. Then buying the cell phone won't put such a dent in your wallet or purse. You can have the phone and still have a lot more money left over.

It's ok if you do your budget or spend plan and discover you don't have enough money for the things you want. That just means that you need to change some things that you are doing. You can either find a way to earn more money and/or cut back on what you are currently spending.

Whether you are still in school and live at home, whether you are a young adult and live at home, if you are an adult out on your own for the first time or whether you are an experienced adult that needs a little help with managing your money, regardless if you are 15 or 50, the concepts and terms in this book are not meant to scare or overwhelm you. I just want you to understand common terms in the financial world and the options that are available to you so you can successfully work toward any financial goal you may have. Knowledge is power!

Chapter 2 -- Set up your 'Ha Ha' Account

It's really just an emergency fund. I like to call it a Ha Ha account for this reason: When financial surprises come about (and they will) like car and house malfunctions, job loss, unexpected medical bills, your dream job requires you to relocate, your identity is stolen and you have to use your backup resources while the matter gets straightened out, and on and on. You will be able to look those surprises in the face and say Ha Ha! I have the money to take care of this without having to borrow and go into debt. How much you need to set aside depends on a variety of personal factors but you do NEED to be adequately prepared for a financial emergency.

Make Yourself Priority #1

When you make yourself a priority you consider that you need to do things to preserve your good health and mental and emotional stability. An emergency fund or a Ha Ha account provides a way to avoid sleepless nights and keep your stress level down. A surprise financial emergency will already threaten your well-being and cause stress and you do not want to add to your list of worries by not having the money to deal with a crisis.

You can also help your mental and emotional well-being by not being forced into making bad financial decisions by increasing credit card debt, borrowing from family or friends (Ugh!) or taking out high interest loans.

How Much Should I Have in an Emergency Fund?

Well . . . it depends, mostly on your age and your position in life at the moment. If you are an adult with your own place to live, most experts believe you should have enough money in your emergency fund to cover at least *3 to 6 months* of living expenses. <u>NOTE</u>: It usually takes an individual more than 3 months to find another job after a loss and begin receiving paychecks again. If you are a young adult, your emergency fund could consist of enough to cover an unexpected car repairs and car insurance premium if you lose your job. If you are a teenager, your emergency fund could be 1/3 of your birthday and Christmas money you've saved over time. This is a good place to start, however, and you can expand later if the need arises.

Start by estimating your costs for critical expenses, such as:

- Housing
- Food
- Health care (including insurance)
- Utilities
- Transportation

- Personal expenses
- Debt

It is not easy to have to spend money to live and save money at the same time, especially if your salary is not at the higher levels BUT it is ***possible and necessary*** for everyone to save if you ever plan on being financially successful. Savings grow over time and even if you're only saving smaller amounts, it will eventually build to something you will be proud of. I cover *Savings and Investments* in more detail a little later on.

Where to Keep the Money

The fund should be placed in a *liquid* account that can be accessed when the emergency occurs (see types of accounts above). A *liquid* account is said to be an account that is easy to sell or convert into cash without any loss in its value. By definition, savings accounts, money market accounts and checking accounts are the most liquid assets. The account should be kept separately from accounts used to pay bills for one reason: <u>To make it inconvenient for you to use</u>. If you think of reasons to use that money like a new flat screen TV or tickets to a concert, you'll end up with a $0 balance. We don't want that. Your account should be liquid, inconvenient for you to access and safe from risk. Your money needs to be there when you need it. As you begin to understand investment principles, it may be alluring to you to put that money into a high interest investment. I'm not suggesting that you reject interest, but make sure you don't risk losing your Ha Ha account.

Chapter 3 – Understand Credit

Credit is the ability to obtain goods and services before you have to pay for it based on the trust that payment will be made in the future. It is basically a loan that involves money that you have to pay back, most often with interest. It can be extremely helpful or harmful depending on how it's used. Once you have credit, you begin to build a credit history. Lenders and landlords use your credit history to measure your ability to repay. Sometimes employers look at it to make a judgment on your 'employability' (whether or not they will hire you). So, a good or bad credit history can make a big difference in getting the loan you need, an apartment you like, the automobile you want or the job of your dreams. Your ability to understand credit and how it can work for or against you is critical in maintaining your financial success.

Credit is offered in several forms such as:

Installment or term loans: With an installment loan, you borrow a specific dollar amount from a lender and you agree to pay the loan back, plus *interest*, in a series of monthly payments. Interest is basically *more money*. You borrow money for a home, a school loan, a business or credit card use and you will have to pay that money back along with a little extra. The extra money is *interest*.

You agree to pay a fixed monthly payment over the length of the loan term, as with student and automobile loans. You don't get additional credit as you pay down the loan, however.

Revolving credit: Revolving credit is a type of credit that does *not* have a fixed number of payments, in contrast to installment credit. Credit cards are an example of revolving credit. When you get a credit card, you're offered funds that you can continually use, up to your established limit, as you pay down the balance. Interest accrues (grows) on the money you borrow until you pay it back.

Mortgage: A mortgage is a loan in which your house functions as the collateral. The bank or mortgage lender loans you a large amount of money which you must pay back -- with interest -- over a set period of time. If you fail to pay back the loan, the lender can take your home through a legal process known as foreclosure.

Establishing Credit

Without credit history, it's hard to qualify for a credit card. But if you start at the bottom and use credit responsibly, you can slowly work your way up to an excellent credit score. It is _extremely important_ to maintain a good credit history throughout your life. The activities below can help you establish credit:

- Acquiring a credit card in your name, for example, Visa®, MasterCard®, American Express®, or Discover®
- Acquiring retail or gas cards, which can be easier to qualify for than a bank card (but don't go crazy and get a lot of these cards – they often have higher interest rates)
- Getting a loan (such as a student loan or an auto loan) in your name, with or without a cosigner or co-applicant

Once you have established credit, lenders use your **credit score** to determine your financial trustworthiness.

Credit Score and Monitoring

Your credit score is a three-digit number resulting from detailed information about your credit history, and it can be one of your most valuable assets. Credit reports explain what you do with your credit. They state when and where you applied for credit, who you borrowed the money from, and who you still owe. Your credit score will play an important role in your financial future: it can mean the difference between being able to purchase a home with a mortgage or having to continue renting. It can also drastically affect the rate of interest you pay on your loans. The higher (and better) your credit score, the less interest (extra money) you will have to pay each month and overall.

The FICO score is the most commonly used credit scoring model. Your FICO score is made up of these five factors:

- *Payment history (35%):* It's important to make your payments on time. Late payments can hurt your credit score and cost you in fees and penalty interest rates.
- *Total Owed (30%):* Keeping your debt balances low in relation to your credit limits is important for good credit health. Generally, you should keep your credit utilization below 30%. And remember, balances are often reported mid-billing cycle, so it's a good idea to keep your utilization below 30% at all times. Consider charges on your credit card as if they are deductions from your checking account.
- *Length of credit history (15%):* The longer your credit history, the better because potential lenders will see you as more creditworthy. Your length of credit history is calculated based on the age of your newest account, the age of your oldest account, and the average age of all of your credit accounts.

- ***Types of credit (10%):*** The mix of different credit accounts (such as auto loans or mortgages) you have will impact your credit in a small way. As a general rule, diversification is better than having only one type of credit account.
- ***New credit/inquiries (10%):*** Applying for too many credit accounts at once can bring your score down. Each new credit application results in a new credit penalty, so try to avoid applying for multiple accounts in a short period of time.

I cannot state this loudly enough. . . .are you ready?. . . **KEEP YOUR CREDIT CARD DEBT LOW!!!!!! AND PAY YOUR BILLS ON TIME!!!!!!**

In the United States, there are three major credit bureaus: *Experian, Trans Union and Equifax.* The credit reporting agencies collect and maintain the information that forms your credit history and ultimately, your credit report. That includes information about your existing credit accounts as well your payment history from a variety of financial institutions, including credit card companies, banks, rental histories, mortgage companies and other lenders. You are entitled to one free credit report per year from each of the three credit bureaus so you can effectively monitor your credit. Your credit report won't contain your credit score (only your history) but you can purchase a credit report with your FICO credit score from any of the three credit bureaus.

As there are three different credit reporting bureaus, you need to check all three of your reports for errors. The information on your reports is used to calculate your credit score, so if there are errors, these errors can keep you from obtaining credit or getting positive credit terms.

Using Credit Responsibly

Credit can be a great financial tool when it is used wisely. Many times people use credit irresponsibly. Credit cards become a problem when we purchase items on impulse, buy things we cannot afford, or live a lifestyle that is way above our means. Depending on your financial situation when your bill arrives, it may be tempting to only pay the minimum amount on your credit card. As tempting as that may be, **DON'T DO IT**. If you can't pay your bill in full, pay as much as you can above the minimum payment. Interest charges can pile up very quickly, and in some cases you may even wind up paying far more than your original balance. All interest charges can usually be avoided by paying the balance in full within the time limit specified on your bill or statement. It is important to get in the habit of using credit responsibly. The first step in establishing this habit is to understand the cost of credit.

Example: Did you know that if you had a balance of $500.00 on your credit card and only paid the minimum balance every month, it would take you almost seven years to pay it off? The total interest would end up costing you $404.64. That means your $500.00 purchase on your credit card actually cost you $904.64! (*This calculation is based on a minimum payment of 3% of the balance and 1.75% interest per month – actual bank rates will vary*).

Cash Advances – Some credit cards offer cash advances. The issuing bank or financial institution treats cash advances like loans, not like purchases of merchandise. When you take out a cash advance using your credit card, interest begins to accrue differently - sometimes without a grace period and at a higher interest rate. Pay close attention to the details and terms of your credit card contract.

Loans

One of the most important factors to consider when selecting a loan is the interest rate. Interest, once again, is the extra money you pay for the privilege of borrowing money. To aid comparison-shopping and eliminate hidden costs, lenders are required to specify the interest rate as an *annual percentage rate (APR)*. The APR includes the interest rate plus all fees and costs, expressed on an annual basis. Choosing a loan with a lower APR will save you money.

An APR may be fixed or variable:

- A **fixed APR** is a specified percentage rate that does not change during the life of the loan. Most vehicle loans and mortgages have a fixed APR.

- A **variable APR** is usually specified as a certain percentage over a moving index. Some credit cards, home equity loans/lines of credit, and mortgages have a variable APR. Monthly payments on variable rate loans can fluctuate, so it is important to understand your loan agreement when considering this type of loan.

To demonstrate how the interest rate (and credit status) affects the cost of a loan, here is an example:

Brian wants to purchase a car for $27,000. He has a down payment of $2,000, so he needs to borrow $25,000. The dealership will finance the car at an APR of 4.32 (good credit) percent and at an APR of 9.5 percent (bad credit). Let's calculate the cost of the loan and the monthly payments.

	Example 1 Good Credit	Example 2 Bad Credit
Auto Loan Amount	$25,000	$25,000
Term	4 years	4 years
Interest Rate	**4.32%**	**9.50%**
Monthly Payment	$603	$667
Total Interest Paid	$3,944	$7,016

As you can see, the interest rate and credit rating affects the amount of the monthly payment and the total amount of interest paid over the life of the loan. That's why comparison shopping for good interest rates and keeping your credit score in good standing is extremely important. (*Actual rates will vary*).

Student Loans

Wikipedia's definition of a student loan is this: A ***student loan*** is designed to help students pay for university tuition, books, and living expenses. It may differ from other types of loans in that the interest rate may be substantially lower and the repayment schedule may be deferred while the student is still in school.

America's overwhelming amount of student debt, as I write this is approximately at $1.2 trillion, and has created a disturbing new phenomenon: School loans that span multiple generations within families. Weighed down by their own loans, many parents lack the means to fund their children's educations without sinking even deeper into debt. Generation X adults — those from 35 to 50 years old — owe about as much as people fresh out of college do. Generation-X parents who carry student debt and have teenage children have struggled to save for their children's educations.

With all this being said (or written as it were), I understand the importance of a good college education. However, please understand that if you rack up $40,000 in student loans and graduate only to find a job making $45,000, or even worse, not being able to find a job at all, you are going to be paying that loan for the rest of your adult life. I know you have to start somewhere, but you will start out way behind the 8-ball this way. Let me offer some things to consider:

- *Example*: If you have $30,000 in student loan debt at 4.29% deferred, but amortized over 6 years; your monthly payment will be $473. If you add that to apartment rent (or mortgage), a car payment, food, utilities, etc. It will get pretty expensive. If you don't make the salary to cover it, you will have to have roommates, live with Mom and Dad or some other arrangement that may not be desirable. Just food for thought.
- If you attend a community college for two years (make sure your credits will transfer over to a university you plan to attend), you will have to borrow a lot less money. Once you transfer over to a university you will still earn the same degree. It will still be a four-year degree from the university of your choosing. Just a lot less debt.
- If you are set on attending a university from the beginning, look to study something that you can *specialize* in. I cannot stress this enough. Employers are overrun with employees who have general skills. If you

want to be marketable, you have to specialize in something. Engineers and nurses don't appear to have a hard time finding gigs. Pick a focus and focus on it. That way, when you graduate you at least have a better than average chance of getting a job and a salary that can chip away at the student loan debt.

- Again, as I write this, some of the most in demand jobs and growing occupations are as follows: *(Some, not all, of these career require a 4 year degree)*.
  - Industrial/Organizational Psychologists
  - Interpreters and Translators
  - Nurses
  - Truck Drivers
  - Market Research Analysts
  - Information Technology Managers
  - Software Development Managers
  - Actuaries
  - Biomedical Engineers
  - Cost Estimators
  - Occupational Therapy Assistants

That is just a short list of the fastest growing jobs in the midst of off the job layoffs, outsourcing and cutbacks that you hear about so often.

If you are Already in Debt

If spending is already a problem for you or you think it might be, the last thing you want to do is slide further into financial trouble by using credit foolishly. It is also not a great idea to hide from debt. The longer you wait to deal with it, the more difficult the problem will become.

Refer back to Chapter 1 of this book. The first thing you need to do is create a household spending plan so you can see *exactly* how much you are in the red. If you owe $100 or so more per month than your take home income, you can probably trim some fat in your spending plan to accommodate that. For instance, you may not need a $4 cup of coffee every morning or 3 pay movie channels on cable or take lunch to work. You can also communicate with your creditors to see if they are willing to work with you on a restructured payment plan or skip one or two payments and tack them on at the end of the loan term. You may also be able to get a temporary part-time job until your outstanding debt is paid

If at the end of your pay cycle or month you are swimming in hundreds or thousands of dollars of debt, you may want to seek help from QUALIFIED sources. If you do want help from a credit counseling agency, check out the company's credentials first. When you enter a *consumer credit counseling program*, you receive information and education about managing your debt effectively and creating actionable plans to repay your balances. A credit counselor can help you maintain a reasonable budget and may help you establish a debt management plan. Companies that offer debt management plans work with the consumer and creditor to create payment plans. The consumer makes a monthly deposit to the debt management company, and these funds are used to pay creditors.

Not all agencies are legitimate -- some charge excessive fees, fail to perform promised services, or provide bad advice, and sometimes even take your money and run. Once you've got a list of counseling agencies you might do business with, check each one out with your state Attorney General and local consumer protection agency to ensure they have a good reputation. Even that is not a guarantee. The United States Trustee Program also keeps a list of credit counseling agencies approved to provide pre-bankruptcy counseling. Check, check and re-check!

Bankruptcy is the last resort if you just cannot find a way out. For the purposes of this book, I will only tell you what bankruptcy is. I will not go into detail into the legalities of it all because 1) I'd never stop writing and 2) I'm not a lawyer. We are going to look on the positive and rosy side of the fence and assume your financial situation is not quite that this point or hopefully as a result of following the principles in this book, will not get to this point.

Bankruptcy is a federal court process designed to help consumers and businesses eliminate their debts or repay them under the protection of the bankruptcy court. Bankruptcies can generally be described as "liquidation" -- Chapter 7 or "reorganization" -- Chapter 13. Under a Chapter 7 bankruptcy, you ask the bankruptcy court to wipe out (discharge) the debts you owe. Under a Chapter 13 bankruptcy, you file a plan with the bankruptcy court proposing how you will repay your creditors. You must repay some debts in full; others may be repaid only partially or not at all, depending on what you can afford.

Tips and Warnings Wrap Up

Now that you've absorbed all of this great news about credit and loans, below is a list of things to remember while you are out in the big and sometimes confusing world of credit:

<u>Do **NOT**</u>:
- Use your credit cards to pay for everyday necessities because you do not have the cash
- Pay your credit card bills late

- Pay only the minimum payment on your credit card(s); owing is easy, repaying is hard
- Apply for many credit cards at once, your credit score will take a hit
- Spend more money than you would have just to receive a bonus, miles or other perks
- Treat cash advances lightly – they have higher interest rates shorter grace periods
- Max out your credit cards
- Get yourself into a situation where you pay off purchases a year later or longer
- Use money from one credit card to pay off another
- Damage your credit score on frivolous items such as expensive clothing or flat screen TVs
- Get an automobile loan for 6 years or longer
- Default on school loans
- Sweep debt under the rug hoping it will go away. It won't. It will follow you. Forever.

DO:
- Pay your credit card bills on time to build a good credit history
- Pay your credit card bill in full if you can or pay as much as you can toward your unpaid balance

- Understand the interest, terms and conditions of your credit cards and loans
- Keep balances low
- Seek out low and fixed interest rates
- Learn what benefits your card(s) may offer
- Compare credit cards before applying
- Be proactive about your card(s) security to avoid identity theft – keep your card, PIN and security code secure
- Determine a repayment strategy for credit cards and other loans
- Monitor your credit report and score
- Know and control your spending habits
- Open new credit accounts only when needed
- Set up a spending plan and live within it
- Get help with debt if you need it, but do your research!
- Capitalize your student loan and **specialize**
- Make smart choices with auto and other loans – understand what you're signing up for
- Ask questions about anything you don't understand before signing agreements/contracts

Chapter 4 – Control Debt and Bills

We've already discussed credit card debt, but what about your other bills? It's easy to quickly accumulate bills and debt to pay off. Debt will hold you back. If you're stuck in a job you don't like, debt will make you afraid to quit. Have you ever thought of taking some time off to consider a change in lifestyle? Forget about it if you are in debt. You can't because your debt has prevented you from building your savings and requires you to continuously earn more money at a constant pace so that you can pay it off. Add to this all of the little "wants" of our lives, the financed cars and vacations, the planned "needs," such as living expenses and higher education, and possible unplanned "surprises" such as medical emergencies, unemployment and relocation, and it's easy to see how debt grows. You will want to avoid as much unnecessary debt as possible – it will lead to a happier life.

Do You Enjoy Your Freedom?

Debt limits your options by keeping you tied to jobs you don't enjoy. You may have to get a 2nd job you don't enjoy to help pay off high levels of debt. It also limits future spending on items that you really need. If you owe so much money every month, you can no longer purchase necessary items in the future. We become enslaved to the services we must perform to get the money for things we bought months sometimes years ago. The best way to maintain your freedom is to never get caught up in the pressure from overdue bills and multiple creditors in the first place. Here are a few tips:

- Have a spending plan – stay within your spending limits
- Have a savings account – you'll be covered for most emergencies
- Pay cash whenever possible
- Avoid bank overdraft charges by monitoring your bank account regularly
- Compare prices before purchasing major items
- Monitor how many 'subscriptions' you sign up for
- Avoid impulse purchases
- Avoid the buy now and pay later model – it will just prolong debt

Practice Discipline and Emotion Control

Discipline is a necessary skill for proper financial management. Without it you will never acquire or accumulate anything of value. *Discipline* is being able to say no when you need to and be able to put money away instead of spending it. No matter what your financial situation is, you need a goal and a plan. If you want to pay off debt, set a date in which to be debt free and calculate how much money you will need to pay each month. If you're trying to save money, attach an amount and a date to your goal. You need to see real numbers to work towards. Break out your big goals into monthly, weekly, and daily tasks.

Discipline, financial or otherwise, won't happen overnight. It takes practice. One thing I want you to do is to Write Your Expenses Down Daily. This goes along with creating and maintaining your spending plan. Whether you do it with pen and paper or electronically, every day after work or school record all of your expenses.

Emotional spending occurs when you buy something you don't need and, in some cases, don't even really want, as a result of feeling stressed out, bored, under-appreciated, incompetent, unhappy, or any number of other emotions. Emotional spending can severely damage your finances and put real stress on your financial goals and plans. There are two major components in emotional spending. One you'll want to avoid; the other you'll want to employ:

You want to avoid Impulse Buys: An *Impulse Buy* is the buying of goods without planning to do so in advance, as a result of a sudden whim or impulse. It is the arch enemy of your spending plan. We've all done it, of course, and it can be incredibly difficult to stop the urge to buy once it's in our minds. There's a cool new pair of jeans, a great looking purse, or an online gadget that we have to have that won't cost much. But hold your fire! Make yourself wait at least 24 hours, if not longer, before making a decision about whether to buy the item. Sometimes the urge will go away. Other times, if you can budget it out, you can wait and get it in a month. *Example*: If you see a backpack you want for $65 but it's not in your monthly spending plan, just plan savings of an additional $17 out of your next 4 weekly checks (or $33 out of your next 2 bi-weekly checks) and pay cash!

Find Alternative Activities: If spending discipline is a problem for you, limit your time at the mall and online window shopping. There are other things you can do with your time: Go get some exercise, visit a museum, calculate your net worth (you know, something fun)! If that just doesn't sound like a great Saturday, then when you are creating your spending plan, budget for impulse buys. Save a specified amount every payday, in addition to your other savings, so at the end of the month or a few months, you have money to just buy what you see. You can splurge all while still setting limits for yourself. Good times!

Keeping Up with the Joneses

I'm sure you have heard this term before. Despite outward appearances, the Joneses are broke! I know the 'Joneses' seem like they have it going on. More often than not, they don't. They are swamped in student loans, car payments and credit card bills because they thought they could pay it off. It may be hard to watch people that you hang around or work with always with the latest fashion or a new Range Rover every two years but living that lifestyle when you're relying on employment wages is a recipe for disaster. Actual wealthy people don't frivolously spend money. That's why they're wealthy! Try not to create imaginary peers. You are not in competition with anyone but yourself. Live in a way that YOUR means allow.

Chapter 5 – What You Have to Save for Now

Putting some money away regularly is the best way of saving up for expensive things, like a vacation, car, a home or a wedding. It can also be a good way of making sure you have money to pay for emergencies such as needing to replace an expensive household item and not having to rely on credit cards or loans. You should also save money for the long-term, such as buying a home and retirement. It can be difficult to think about doing this, especially when you're young and retirement seems a long way off. It's a good idea to think about whether you'll have enough to live on when you are older and no longer earning money. Pretty much every person knows that saving money is a great thing but not as many people do it or think about all of the benefits from saving. Let me tell you how saving helps YOU:

Happiness

When you know you have money to cover your bills and some unexpected things that will, undoubtedly arise, your level of stress is reduced tremendously. It's nothing worse than being stressed out and up at night worrying about how you are going to pay for something. Low stress level helps you lead a healthier and happier life.

Independence

When you have enough money to fund your own life and cover your own expenses you have a level of financial independence that will let you call your own shots and make choices. You don't have to remain stuck in a bad relationship or living situation or remain in a bad job. You have the freedom to switch careers, take a vacation, invest and retire when you want to.

Keeps you from Overpaying for Things

If you have the cash to pay for normal everyday items, it keeps you from having to use credit to make those purchases and being subject to paying added interest charges on those items.

Retirement

If I only was able to offer one piece of advice, it would be this: Save for Retirement and the Future Now!!! By the time that comes around (even if you're only 18 right now) if you haven't saved enough, you will wish that you had. Contrary to popular belief, you expenses really don't decrease that much when you retire. You basically have the same bills minus commuting costs, work clothing, parking and lunches out. The last thing you want is to be forced to get a part-time job when you're 69 years old because you ran out of money. Ugh!

There are many venues to saving for retirement. Just to name a few –

Traditional Individual Retirement Account (IRA) – If you make contributions to a traditional IRA, it reduces the income that you have left because you take money from your savings to make that contribution. This is a tax deferred account and reduces your income tax bill.

401k – Is a fund set up by your employer. You contribute pre-tax dollars from your salary to fund this account. It reduces the amount of take home pay that you receive. If you're lucky, your employer may add matching funds which will double your savings amount. This is also a tax deferred account and will reduce the amount you have to pay in income taxes.

Example of retirement savings:

- Brian earns $90,000 per year.
- He gets paid on a bi-weekly basis.
- His income tax rate is 28%
- He contributes 8% of his salary to his 401(k) each payday.
- Brian's bi-weekly contributions will be $276
- His paycheck would only be reduced by $199

Let's make it even more basic . . . If you are 20 years old today and you plan to retire at 65. Even if you just invested $50 a week, in one year you would have put away $2,600 ($50 X 52 weeks = $2,600).

In 45 years, those cash deposits alone would add up to $117,000 ($2,600 X 45 = $117,000).

How do you **turn that into a million** you ask? *Interest on Your Investment!*

Every day that your money is invested, it earns interest, then your interest earns interest—and your savings begin to mount.

Assuming your money earns an average of about 8% per year, here's how your savings would grow:

In 10 years you would have $40,000

In 20 years you would have $128,000

In 30 years you would have about $325,000

In 40 years you would have over $764,000

In the 45th year, you would have about $1,001,000

Housing

Buying a Home - You have to have a down payment on a home before the bank will lend you money. 20% is recommended; however, you can get a loan with less money down. You will have to have some of your own money. The more you put down, the less you will have to pay in the long run.

Having savings on hand affords you the opportunity to make purchases when the timing is right for you and being able to take advantage of opportunities as they arise.

I know there is a lot of pressure to buy a home. You hear many financial experts telling you all the benefits of owning. While owning property does create financial security, buying a home should be carefully considered and if you don't feel that it will work for you, don't get pressured into it. ***Renting*** has many benefits as well:

- *Career Flexibility* - If you are renting, you are not locked into your location if the job market or your career preferences change.
- *No Property Taxes* – Your landlord pays all property taxes and basic insurance (you still should get renters insurance).
- *Lower Monthly Cost* – Renting often carries a lower monthly cost overall than owning a home. When you consider mortgage, property tax, insurance, maintenance, and things like association fees, renting can still be less expensive.

- *Lower Maintenance Costs* – If almost anything inside or outside of your unit breaks, your landlord is responsible for fixing it. You don't have to endure the loss of money or time to deal with it.
- *Less Stress* – Renters have less worry about maintenance, the home's value possible decreasing due to a bad market and other issues that go along with owning a home.

Experiences Not Things

Research has shown that purchasing an experience tends to improve your lifestyle and well-being more than purchasing a possession. Experiences create memories and establish valuable connections with others that can possibly help you further down the road. Correct me if I'm wrong but I don't think you will look back on your life and fondly remember that you had the most recent smartphone or the latest trendy shoes.

Keep in mind that things lose value, go out of style, and faze out. Just look at your smartphone. Your experiences become a part of you. The sights you see, the people you encounter and the activities in which you engage are all cherished experiences that cannot be taken away from you. You can look back with photos, videos and your own memory for the rest of your life.

Chapter 6 – You are Never too Young to Invest

Investments

You are never too young to start saving money, investing and planning your financial future. An *investment* in its simplest term is the use of your money in the hope of making more money. It involves the choice by an individual, after some research and analysis, to commit or lend money in a vehicle, instrument or asset, such as property (real estate), stock, bond, commodity, or financial derivative (i.e., futures or options), that has a certain level of risk and provides the possibility of generating additional income (returns) over a period of time.

Investment is an extremely broad subject. There are many kinds of investments, each with its own level of risk and return. The more money you can make from an investment, the higher the risk that you might not get all your money back. I will just gently touch on a few types of investments here.

- 401(k) -Retirement
  Most 401(k) plans provide at least three investment choices in your 401(k) plan, but some plans offer dozens. Some plans offer brokerage accounts, which means you can

select investments from the full range of stocks, bonds, mutual funds, and other types of assets. Every 401(k) plan lets you decide how to invest the contributions you make. Some plans also let you decide how to invest your employer's matching contributions, but others let the employer make that choice.

- Bonds
  A bond is like an IOU issued by the government or a company. You lend them your money for a number of years, and they promise to pay a certain interest rate – called a coupon. The price you will get can go up and down. Bonds are also sometimes called fixed interest investments.

- Shares/Stocks
  When you buy a share, you're buying a small part of a business or company. If that company makes money, you may be paid a share of the profit, called a ***dividend***. Like house prices, share prices are expected to go up over time and give you a 'capital gain' on your money when you sell. However, prices can fall in value as well.

- Property/Real Estate
  Returns from investing in property come from rental income and from any increase in the value of property over time – called capital gain. Some people view their own

home as an investment because it may grow in value. You can also invest in commercial property directly, or through managed funds.

Get a Head Start on Investing with These Simple Steps

1) *Set a goal* – identify short term and long term goals for why you choose to invest and how much money you will need to meet those goals.   Hint: Retirement should be one of your long term goals. Other examples would be a new car, education, or starting a business.

2) *Gauge your risk tolerance* – risk is the uncertain and often scary part of investing. Usually the greater the potential return, the greater the risk you will have to assume. If the thought of constant ups and downs in the market makes you want to pull your hair out, you may want to consider more conservative investments.

3) *Construct your portfolio* – It's like you're the captain of the team and you have the responsibility of choosing the right players. Each member will have their own special strengths but they all will have to work together for the team's good. Start by establishing the broad categories that will make up your portfolio -- stocks versus

bonds, or mutual funds for instance, and then narrow down from there. This is where diversification comes into play. It's good to have diversity in your portfolio.

Diversification is the act of adding a variety of investments to your portfolio to reduce the risk inherent in any one investment.

4) *Put it on automatic pilot* – regular payroll deductions are the most painless way. Have deposits into savings accounts, retirement accounts and investment funds electronically transferred from your check directly to the account. The less you have to do the less overwhelming it will be. Also, this way you won't miss the money if you never see it on your paycheck. You will learn to live on your new net pay. However (and this is a big one), MONITOR YOUR PORTFOLIO at least one every quarter (4 times per year) to check performance and to evaluate whether or not you need to make adjustments.

Low Risk Investment Options

No one wants to lose money. That's what makes low risk investments an attractive option to cautious investors. There are a couple of things to consider though: 1) Low risk investments earn very modest returns 2) The rate of inflation may catch up or outpace what you earn on low risk investments. **Inflation** means the dollar amount will stay the same but each dollar will have less purchasing power over time. If you are a beginner and you can't afford to lose any money or just the thought of sudden swings (and losses) in the stock market make you lose sleep, below are a few low risk options. No investment is completely free from risk. These are by no means an attempt to tell you what to do with your money (you must make that decision for yourself) and they won't make you an overnight millionaire, but your money will grow on some level over time.

1) *Income Mutual Funds* - Income funds invest in a wide range of income-producing instruments, such as bonds, mortgages, senior secured loans, and preferred and utility stocks. The diversification and professional management they offer lessens the market risks found in individual securities. The combination of different classes of securities, such as bonds and preferred stocks, can also combine to provide an above average payout with less risk than individual offerings.

2) *Fixed Annuities* - Fixed annuities are designed for conservative retirement savers who seek higher yields with safety of

principal. These instruments possess several unique features, including: You can put a virtually unlimited amount of money away and let it grow tax-deferred until retirement, their rates are generally about 0.5% to 1% higher than CDs or treasury securities, and the major risks that come with annuities are liquidity risk (due to an early withdrawal penalty).

3) *Municipal Bonds* - What makes municipal bonds so safe? Not only do you avoid income tax (which means a higher return compared to an equally risky investment that is taxed) but they are backed by the government and the likelihood of the borrower defaulting is very low.

No matter what you decide to invest in, I have to stress this point once again, PLEASE DO YOUR RESEARCH so you are comfortable with the terms and conditions, the returns and the risks. Fill out the paperwork to open your first investment account, and begin accumulating the money that will help you accomplish your goals for the future.

Chapter 7 – Pursue and Maximize Benefits

An employee benefit package can mean a lot when it comes to having more money in your pocket. For instance, a lot of recent college graduates think short term and assume that a higher paycheck will benefit them more than a generous benefit package. Maybe and maybe not. More pay does not always equal the best job offer. One of the best ways to ensure you are getting the best offer is to consider and take advantage of your employer's benefit program.

What Benefits Does Your Job Offer?

In most cases, if you are a full time worker, you are eligible for benefits which are part of your total compensation. Employers generally pay for a portion of your benefits and can save you quite a bit of money over the long term.

Medical, dental and vision insurance – these help cover the high and rising cost of health care and will mean fewer out-of-pocket expenses for your future medical, dental and vision needs.

Life Insurance – can be an important part of your overall financial plan especially if you have loved ones who depend on your financial support. It replaces your income if the event that you die.

Flexible Spending Accounts – can pay for medical, dental, vision or even child care expenses on a pre-tax basis.

Retirement plans – As we discussed earlier, retirement plans such as 401(K)s and 403(B)s are a great way to save for retirement with the added benefit of having contributions be tax deferred. Some employers even provide matching contributions to a certain extent.

How to Maximize Your Benefits

Once you know what you have, it's a just a matter of taking advantage of it. The first step would be to understand what is available to you: read your insurance policies to find out what you're entitled to, understand your 401(k) so you can maximize your savings, comprehend your health benefits to know if you have to pay a deductible and how much your-copays will be if you get sick, investigate whether or not your employer has a tuition reimbursement program or how you can get discounted gym membership. There are many benefits and perks offered by companies that don't necessarily include additional salary. But, by the time you maximize all of your available benefits, it can add as much as 25-35% value to your compensation.

Chapter 8 – Important Education Begins Now

Okay, don't get me wrong and please don't send me harsh bashing emails or letters. I am in no way saying that higher education is not necessary or beneficial. It is indeed! I just believe you can only learn so much in school about real life. The schools teach English, math, and science (along with some other stuff), but most Americans will never use the concepts of that teaching in real life situations. While the school may teach a home economics course, they may not teach how to grocery shop on a budget. They may show you how to multiply fractions but they generally don't explain how, why or where to save money. A high GPA may get you a job, but it doesn't help you become successful at managing money or using credit wisely. So, that's why I say that your important education begins now. If you want to be successful and enjoy freedom in living, you must employ many of the strategies described in this book. When your bills are paid and you have money saved for emergencies as well as for the future, you tend to sleep a lot easier.

Personal Development at Every Stage

Never stop learning! Lifelong learning is continuous education and training from cradle to grave involving formal and informal methods of learning. It is important as you go and grow through life to continue to learn and develop your skills. Continuous learning allows for creation of new ideas and new goals and creativity turns problems and challenges into opportunities and solutions. Let me give you quick example: Just say you are in a position where you have a good job, making a good salary, already purchased a home and things are going relatively well. Don't allow that to be the point where you stop and say, 'I've arrived.' This is where you begin to explore where you would like to go next in life. You ask yourself the following questions:

- What skills do I need to advance in my career?
- Do I want to go from wage earner to entrepreneur?
- What skills/activities can I learn to increase my net worth?
- What are the top 5 things I would like to accomplish next?
- What can I do to share my knowledge with others who aren't yet at my level?

Those questions, along with others that I'm sure you will think of, will launch you into the next learning phase of your life. It will give you motivation, self-confidence and self-esteem and will make your experience more purposeful and fulfilling.

Mentors – Get One or Two

The American author, salesman and motivational speaker Zig Ziglar once said, "A lot of people have gone further than they thought they could because someone else thought they could." Don't limit yourself and be reluctant to try new things because of fear or a lack of belief in yourself. No matter your position in life, a good mentor is an invaluable resource in business or in whatever area you choose to succeed.

One concept that I've always believed is that you become like the people you hang around the most. So, if you want to be more successful than you are, you must find, network and learn from people who are living the life you desire. A good mentor will help you stay accountable to your goals, they will help you pay attention and stay on track. When you get frustrated and want to give up they will push you harder and keep you going. A good mentor will help you in your professional life and cut your learning curve tremendously in new projects. If you venture out to learn something on your own, it will take time, trial and error. Having a mentor will significantly reduce the amount of time it takes you to learn and can also help you avoid some (not all) of the trial and error of your new endeavor. A mentor is essential for providing knowledge, motivation, advice and counsel, encouragement when you need it most, help with personal development and so much more.

Now that you know a little more than your school taught you about money, I wish you all the personal discipline, luck and success in the world to continue on your journey.

www.ingramcontent.com/pod-product-compliance
Lightning Source LLC
Chambersburg PA
CBHW040848180526
45159CB00001B/357